Valley Stream In Pictures

Summer Edition

by

Marc Zirogiannis

Zirogiannis, Marc

Valley Stream In Pictures

Summer Edition

 62 pages

ISBN 978-1725543386

Marc Zirogiannis

Valley Stream, NY 11580

Inquiries or additional information contact

redflagadvisors@gmail.comor visit our website:
http://www.lulu.com/spotlight/ZIRO11801

THIS BOOK IS DEDICATED TO MY BOYS

About The Author

Marc Zirogiannis holds a B.A. from Long Island University and a *Juris Doctor* from Hofstra University's School of Law. Mr. Zirogiannis is a world renowned Business Development Consultant and Author. Mr. Zirogiannis has practiced the martial arts for over 25 years and earned a 3rd Dan under the supervision of Grandmaster Yeon Hwan Park in Levittown, New York.

He has been active in practicing and teaching meditation for 10 years. He has published numerous books, eBooks, and Audio Books an on a variety of subjects, and, is currently the Editor in Chief for **Tae Kwon Do Life Magazine**, an international print publication. He lectures on a variety of topics, including business development, personal development, and matters of the martial arts.

His last novella, **Hitler's Orphan: Demetri of Kalavryta,** has won critical acclaim and been the subject of a radio program. It is currently in negotiations to become the basis of a more extensive work.

His latest works **The Suffering of Innocents** (2015) and **The Rise and Fall of H&H Bagels** (2016) were released by *Revival Waves of Glory Books & Publishing* and have been a critical successes.

Acknowledgements

I came to Valley Stream almost, and only, two years ago. Having lived on Long Island and Queens most of my life I knew of the Village and Town but never thought too much of it. All I knew was what I had read in the newspaper, and saw on TV, in December of 1990 about the terrible **Godfather 3** murders at the Green Acres Mall. That tragedy negatively shaped my view of the area.

Cut to 27 years later and I end up in this beautiful and embracing neighborhood with my beloved family. I am thankful to have made it here eventually.

The neighborhood is rich with history and scenery and a warmth unmatched in any of the places I have resided or visited.

Special thanks to Joseph Pontillo and his entire family for sharing his love of Valley Stream with me and helping to welcome me.

Marc A. Zirogiannis

Valley Stream in Pictures

<u>**Be sure to visit:**</u>

The Valley Stream Train Station

The Valley Stream Dog Park

The Henry Waldinger Memorial Library

Valley Stream's Village Hall

The Cigar Superstore

Arthur Hendrickson Park & Pool Complex

The 9/11 Memorial

Howell Road Elementary School

The Brookside Deli Shopping Center

The Valley Stream State Park

Nick's Service Center (formerly Joyal)

Sip This

The LIJ-Northwell Hospital at Valley Stream

Ali Baba's

Ralph's Italian Ices

Green Acres Mall

Fireman's Field (on the 4th of July)

VILLAGE of VALLEY STREAM
INCORPORATED 1925

...GE of VALLEY STREAM
LOYAUTÉ M'OBLIGE
ON THE TRAIL OF THE RISING SUN
INCORPORATED 1925

Trains
Ahead
Tickets

VALLEY
STREAM
FIRE
DEPARTMENT
OFFICE SUP

VALLEY
STREAM
FIRE
DEPARTMENT
DEDICATED TO THOSE WHO HAVE ANSWERED THEIR LAST ALARM AND
HAVE MADE THE SUPREME SACRIFICE IN SERVICE TO OUR COMMUNITY.

"EVERY DOG MUST HAVE HIS
- Jonathan S
TERMINATED.
PARKING FOR DOG PARK
MONDAY THRU FRIDAY
LIBRARY PARKING LOT

HENRY WALDINGER
MEMORIAL LIBRARY

WALLACE HALL

ILLAGE HALL
VALLEY STREAM

Long Island
Rail Road
ONE WAY

CIGAR
SUPERSTORE
← Satte
Brooklyn
NEXT S
ONE WAY
NISSAN

VALLEY STREAM
DAKTRONICS
CLASSIC CAR SHO
THURSDAY EVENINGS
PARKING FIELD #12
MINEOLA & FAIRVIEW
YOUR OFFICIAL VILLAGE INFORMATION CEN
PLEASE CALL 825-4200
SALE

WELCOME
TO BEAUTIFUL
HENDRICK
K & POOL COM
HE MANY PARK & RECREATIONAL
ADHERE TO THE FOLLOWING RE
COHOL, CAMPFIRES, EXPLOSIVES, FIREA
DING WILDLIFE, LOITERING AFTER 11 P.M., LITT
S, SOLICITING, SMOKING, VANDALISM, UNAUTH
HAVE A GREAT TIME!
MAYOR
EDWIN A. FARE
TRUSTEES
TUFARELLI
M. GRASSO
GE JUSTICE
DERMON
SEAN
VIRGINIA CLAVIN

WELCOME
THIS PLAYGROUND HAS BEEN
DESIGNED FOR CHILDREN
2-5 YEARS OLD
ADULT SUPERVISION
IS RECOMMENDED
Miracle

VALLEY STREAM
POOL

In Memory of
Linda A. Santisteban
Always in our Hearts

well Road Scho
rking Together to Make Things Happ

SALON II
BARBER SHOP
OPEN 24 HRS
PHOTO
RITE AID
PHARMACY

ALLEY STREAM
TATE PARK
BALLFIELDS
SOUTHERN STATE PKWY.
TOLLBOOTH
BASKETBALL COURT
HORSESHOE PIT
PARK OFFICE-POLICE
SQUIRREL HUT TRAIL
PKWY. EAST
RESTROOM
GARDEN AREA
SWING SET
2-5 PLAYGROUND
CHALLENGER 5-12 PLAYGROUND
PAVILION-PICNIC AREA
PICNIC AREA
FLETCHER AVE.
CORONA AVE.
SERVICE ROAD
RESTROOM
YOU ARE HERE
HANDICAP TABLE
FIRE HYD.
HICKORY HUT TRAIL
HENDRICKSON AVE.
NEW YORK STATE
Par
and
Pre

NICK'S
SERVICE CENTER
Family O

Sip This
RESSO · SMOOTHIES · PASTRIES · EN

Long Island Jewish
Valley Stream
Northwell Health

← Blakeman
Field Visitor
Parking

BQ
GYR

ITALIAN ICES • ICE CREAM
FAMOUS
SHAKES • SMOOTHIES • SUNDAES

green
acres
mall